Answer Then Question
Haikus and Other Poems

Ian Ebbitt

SAKURA PUBLISHING
Hermitage, Pennsylvania
USA

Answer Then Question

Haikus and Other Poems

by
Ian Ebbitt

Answer Then Question:
Haikus and Other Poems
Copyright © 2013 by Ian Ebbitt
All rights reserved. Published in the United States by Sakura Publishing in 2013. No part of this publication may be reproduced, distributed, or transmitted in any form or by any means, including photocopying, recording, or other electronic or mechanical methods, without the prior written permission of the publisher, except in the case of brief quotations embodied in critical reviews and certain other noncommercial uses permitted by copyright law. For permission requests, write to the publisher, addressed "Attention: Permissions Coordinator," at the address below.
Sakura Publishing
PO BOX 1681
Hermitage, PA 16148
www.sakura-publishing.com

Ordering Information:
Quantity sales: Special discounts are available on quantity purchases by corporations, associations, and others. For details, contact the publisher at the address above. Orders by U.S. trade bookstores and wholesalers. Please contact Sakura Publishing: Tel: (330) 360-5131; or visit www.sakura-publishing.com.

Book Cover and Interior Design by Rania Meng

First Edition

Printed in the United States of America

ISBN-13: 978-0-9911807-2-1

ISBN-10: 0991180720

Dedication

This book is dedicated to three magnificent people:

To my mother, Cheryle, who has always supported me in all of my crazy endeavors without hesitation. Thank you for believing in me, repeatedly.

To my grandmother, Winifred, who has given me the 'rhyming gene'.

To my grandmother, Jane, to whom I never had the privilege of meeting in person because of her young death but who has given me strength and a good nature. I know this because of the vivid and accurate picture my father has painted for me in my mind since I was very young.

Acknowledgement

There are many, many people I would like to thank, but in an effort to keep this short I will only name the most important one.

I would like to thank the Lord Jesus Christ. For anything you may enjoy about me or what I write, it all comes from his hands. Without Him, I am nothing.

Parker,

If you do not care for the shape of your future, mold and create a better one.

Love,
Dad

Chapter 1
Haiku For You

Haiku For You
_____

A GREAT MOMENT...

Mouth wide, looking up
He's only seven months old!
My boy kisses me

Haiku For You

ANGLER'S DAY...

Scent of salty sea
Strong, slimy hands, wet red boots
A regular day

Haiku For You

ANSWER THEN QUESTION...

Does the Lord love me?
The answer already there
My son was my proof

Haiku For You

ARGYLE...

Old Scot perspective
Symmetrical lozenges
Timeless golfer style

Haiku For You

BEGINNING OF SUMMER...

Fragrance of downed rain
Dog, old tent, bark of a pine:
What I remember

Haiku For You

FRIDAY HAPPY HOUR : PART 1...

A supportive stool
Flavored ice chased with spirits
The first sip lingers

Haiku For You

Answer Then Question

FRIDAY HAPPY HOUR : PART 2...

Thoughts are left behind
Friends share stories of the week
Woes erased for now

Haiku For You

HARA KIRI...

An Eastern belief
Change dishonor to honor
Slow pain self-inflict

Haiku For You

LAS VEGAS TRUTH...

Immorality
Sin blanketed in good times
Devil won this one

Haiku For You

LUCKIEST CLOVER...

Hiding in mixed grass
Can' t quite tell, three leaves or four
I still feel lucky

Haiku For You

MARCH 25, 2013...

White sinks towards us
Quiet, slowly, peacefully:
Heaven meets Pittsburgh

Haiku For You

MODUS OPERANDI...

Window and a note
A working class neighborhood
Oh Damn! Arrested

MOTHER'S HAND PREVAILS...

Rhythmic, gentle, soft
Comfort in a stroking hand
Infant quick asleep

Haiku For You

MY NIGHT, MY FIGHT...

Sweat, nerves, hide my fear
Enter a fenced arena
One hand will be raised

Haiku For You

NOT FINISHED...

Time, never enough
Plant time. Grow time. Need more time.
Not quite done with my

Haiku For You

PENNSYLVANIA FALL...

Windows frosted shut
Cup of tea clutched in my hands-
The warm in the cold

RECOVERY...

Solitude in pain
A journey I take alone
Yesterday again

Haiku For You

RED BALLOON ALIVE...

Dance without a floor
Motion of silent music
Balloon is alive

Haiku For You

SHAMROCK FAITH...

Luck of the Shamrock
Shamrock shows more than just luck
Catholics know better

SPRING BOUND...

The white becomes less
Water washes the grasses
Winter disappears

TAXES...

My money goes where-
Hand over fist, allocate
Our thief stole from me

Haiku For You

THAT TIME AGAIN...

Not leap year but four
Crooks congregate to speak out
Election is here

Haiku For You

TIME LOST...

Where, why, what, when, how
Wide-eyed faces crowd the bed
From coma I woke

TOO LATE - GONE...

Words thought but not said
Silence. But I did love you
I should have said it

Haiku For You

WHY RIGHT NOW? ...

No don' t. Don' t leave me!
Why do you choose now to go?
Indiscretions found

Haiku For You

BEGINNER PUGILIST ...

Hands up, chin down, move?
More radiating head pain
Must learn to parry

Haiku For You

JIU JITSU REALITY...

Uncomfortable
Concerned, pain, my skills kick in
I won' t tap today

Haiku For You

A BIKER UNDERSTANDS...

Sweeping turns, steep cliffs
Motorcycle's paradise
Tail of the Dragon

Haiku For You

TOOLS OF THE TRADE...

Helmet, head lamp, pick
Bravery with confidence
Coal miner' s checklist

Haiku For You

VISTA OFTEN MISSED...

Taken for granted
Pink and lavender fall sky
Appalachia

A WINNER'S MINDSET...

Slow, steady climb up
Success awaits at the top
I will peer down soon

OUR END IS NEAR...

Little yellow friend
Canary dies suddenly
Coal miner's worst fear

Limericks To Like

Chapter 2
Limericks To Like

BE A PATRIOT...

Soldiers provide us our freedom
Thanks for the efforts that lead them
So pick up your flag
And begin to brag
Show gratitude whenever you see them

Limericks To Like

BIG CHUCK...

There once was a cow named Big Chuck
Who seemed to be plagued with bad luck
He tried to escape
But too wide in his shape
In the fence is where he got stuck

Limericks To Like

BIG OL' PETEY...

You can see in his eyes he was proud
As Petey drew in a large crowd
He stood a squared stance
Then unzipped his pants
Big Petey was quite well endowed

Limericks To Like

BIRTH CURSE...

I was born with a bit of a curse
I speak in a rhyme and a verse
You say that it's great
I argue that fate
My word, it is getting much worse

Limericks To Like

Answer Then Question

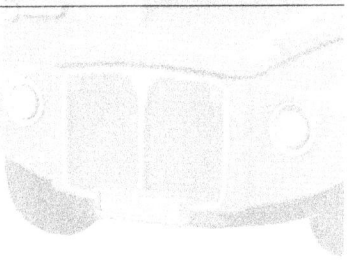

CLAUSTROPHOBIA...

Things quickly began to go wrong
The moment I stepped in a throng
It's getting harder to breathe
All I want is to leave
Two minutes is two minutes too long

Limericks To Like

DOG'S BEST FRIEND...

The dog started spinning around
Appeared to be gaining some ground
It chased a new friend
Again and again
New friend was its tail that it found

Limericks To Like

FARMER'S RESOLVE...

Fred was needing some eggs to sell
But his chickens weren' t laying that well
He gripped up two hens
He squeezed them and then
Plop, plop went two eggs that then fell

Limericks To Like

FIX YOUR FASHION...

I appeared to be looking a mess
My wardrobe was not a success
I ran to the store
I spent a bit more
But damn, I look good in this dress!

Limericks To Like

FORGETFUL BOY...

There once was a boy who forgot
He could not remember a lot
He paused in his walk
And paused in his talk
Turns out he forgot his next thought

IMPOTENCE CURED...

Faulty in his lower man section
Caught sight of her curvy perfection
A tingle and a smile
Only took a short while
Hooray! He regained his erection!

Limericks To Like

IT'S HERE, IT'S GONE...

In the distance I see a storm falling
Now closer I hear the storm calling
It strikes in a blink
With no time to think
The damage is really appalling

Limericks To Like

LISTEN SIMON LISTEN...

It seems Simon was told something twice
Not sure why the first did not suffice
He picked the wrong guys
They blackened both of his eyes
Hopefully next time he'll take their advice

Limericks To Like

MISSED OPPORTUNITY...

Began with an awkwardly dance
Quickly realized he missed his last chance
Some pressure in his tummy
Then a push on his bummy
Oh dear someone soiled their pants!

Limericks To Like

MORALE BOOSTER...

Morale has been steadily sinking
I have a solution I'm thinking
Let's all move fast
Grab a fifth and a glass
We'll fix it by everyone drinking

Limericks To Like

MY MARILYN...

It began with a strong wind that was blowing
Then her long, white dress started flowing
We didn' t tell her until after
We enjoyed some good laughter
That for a moment her flower was showing

Limericks To Like

PATIENCE LEFT THE BUILDING...

Did her own taxes to save her some dough
But miscalculated what she would owe
She filed her last claim
Stood on the ledge and took aim
Patience screamed till she hit the sidewalk below

PLEASE DON'T DRIVE...

There was an old lady who would drive
I think she was a hundred and five
Too little to see
Which lane she should be
It's a wonder that she's still alive

Limericks To Like

PROBLEM SOLVER...

There is something I have to confess
My boss has been causing me stress
I bought a new gun
Bang, bang it was done
Suddenly my stress is much less

Limericks To Like

RESURRECTION STORY...

His miracles always amaze
And he never renounced his ways
For that he was beaten
But certainly not weakened
For he rose from the tomb in three days

STRAIGHTEN UP THE DAY...

My day was not going so great
It began when I woke up too late
I' m beginning to wilt
I now walk with a tilt
I should have had a V8

Limericks To Like

THAT PIZZA...

The smell of that pizza is nice
I think I'll go grab me a slice
I'll take two of them please
Both with bacon and cheese
I'll probably get back in line twice

Limericks To Like

THE DENTIST IS NOT MY FRIEND...

I took a bite of my apple at lunch
Then a sharp pain with an echoing crunch
"Please Doc, help my tooth!"
"Here' s the straight ugly truth,
I am going to pull out a bunch."

Limericks To Like

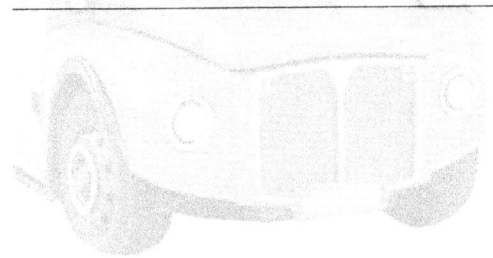

TODAY, MY BOY...

I sit in a room as I wait
No schedule but I think he is late
She pushes so long
There's a faint crying song
The birth of my son is just great

Limericks To Like

TSK TASK...

He was born to perform just one task
It's obvious there's no need to ask
You hear his words mumble
You see his feet stumble
Excuse me whilst I drink from my flask

Limericks To Like

WORKING GAL...

There once was a gal named Dolores
She would do anything for us
She worked off her knees
Charging nominal fees
My, she had quite the clitoris

A Bit More Mature

Chapter 3
A Bit More Mature

A Bit More Mature

A TAKEN MAN...

I once lived a life, a really good life
With a cute cloned-me son and a witty trophy wife
A secure job, a cool motorcycle, and a wonderful house
A house on a dead end street
A house with a large yard
With a creek in the back
And a koi pond off the patio with a waterfall.
I had friends and family that filled my life space hand over fist.
The people that cared about me, I'm gracious to say, was an extensive list.
My days were long, but in an appreciative way.
I wanted not for anything on this heavenly Earth.
I sang the song the whole world wanted to sing.
Past tense.
Notice everything is in the past tense.
Where am I now?
Taken.
What was the change in my life's course events?
Though I cannot pinpoint the moment,
The exact moment,
I know when.
It was the moment Greed knocked on my door

A Bit More Mature

And like a blind fool I opened the door.
I should not just say I opened the door.
I welcomed him in with open arms.
Why?
I'm not sure exactly.
Maybe it was his charismatic way
His enthusiastic promises to a better future
The way he tapped into my yearning for respect
The kind of respect that can only be achieved with power.
He polished my desire to be the vantage of envy
Knowing that secretly I wanted to judge instead of be judged.
Drew my belief that the grass is greener on the other side of the fence,
Greed's side of the fence.
Well, anyhow it worked.
It more than worked.
I became a conductor orchestrating a symphony of Greed's work.
Accolades to the level I achieved of greed.
Tunnel vision,
Complete and total tunnel vision,
So much so that I cannot begin to recall the time of my losses.
No, not tangible losses
The losses of untouchables
Relationships, empathy, caring, reciprocity,

Self, perspective, generosity, and human decency.
Not to worry though
I never lost love.
The love is still there.
It did on the other hand morph
Changing to a love of all things that rot
That rots a person from the inside out.

A Bit More Mature

AMERICA THE BEAUTIFUL...

Ha Ha
Pay homage to me
I am the pinnacle of what you should be
My assembly line productivity is at an all-time high
With corruption and deception from floor to sky
My created clones will alter the future of society
A beautiful thing, my propriety
We look faceless so that we may blend in
To rot today's values from deep, deep within
Take, take, take
It is never enough
My corporate clones walk on the heads of blue collars
When times get tough
'Better you than me' has always been my motto
You suckers stay poor as I sit on a winning lotto
Ah yes greed
It makes the world go round
The ching in rising costs of living is a most beautiful sound
We rise to the top as the market crashes below
I couldn't care less about you so long as my pockets grow
False prophecy, who cares
I'm the one on the pedestal
You lower class nobodies can keep your comments of

ridicule
The propensity to propagandize
Untruths and lies
Blah Blah Blah
No one up top can hear the little people's cries
I suppose all is well that ends well
Now please mail my check to 666 Hell

BLONDE INNOCENCE...

Skin shades of light
Eyes large and bright
Finger nails petite
Chubby little feet
Smell of sinless
Soft cheeks caress
Cynicism unknown
Far from grown
Inability to lie
Honesty in a cry
Silly brings smiles
Unconditional for miles
All new exposures
Unfiltered disclosures
Sleep and play the norm
Before bad habits form
Early in life
Absence of strife
No ulterior motive
But cuteness effective
Unaware of manipulation
God' s perfect creation
Body without a mark

A Bit More Mature

Hair not yet dark
Before common sense
Blonde innocence

CLARITY COMES AT THE BOTTOM OF A FIFTH...

I think back to a time of troubled days
Walking through life in a cotton thick haze
Weeks bled together in a trance-like daze

Where I once was fully capable
Every thought had become imponderable
My mind and body had taken quite a toll

No longer could I recognize, conceptualize, or visualize
Things that I use to be able to surmise or at the very least realize
Were replaced with lost thoughts and night filled cries

Was it a rarity that I found clarity or was it a myth?
That I found clarity at the bottom of a fifth

A Bit More Mature

END TABLE...

Sparkle in your eyes
Kiss at the door
Days start to blend
Lucky to be greeted anymore
    Valentines', anniversaries
    Planned in advance and with love
    Now you rush out for a gift
    No sooner than the day of
Mornings were coffee
And heart to heart chat
Now it's just coffee
What happened to that?
    Bed fit like a single
    Sleeping close to my friend
    Now I barely see you
    Way at the other end
We were once as one
Traveling in the same direction
Your looking away when we talk
Was my first detection
    Earlier to work
    Later to return
    Why now does it take longer
    To receive the same earn?

A Bit More Mature

I begin to grow suspect
For good reason, not sure
I go to bed at eleven
But stare at the ceiling till four
    I have two eyes
    One is on you
        Can this be happening?
        Can this be true?
First it was denial
Then I grew wise
I see the decay
In our marital demise
    In three life times
        I would have never thought you able
        The door closes gently behind me
        The ring is on the end table

I DROVE TO HEAVEN ON AN ASPHALT ROAD...

I was off to work one morning
On the same course I usually go
When the sunlight peeked out in warning
It illuminates the heavens you know

Mesmerized as I caught the view
My destination permanently altered
Off I went into the still sky blue
Asking forgiveness for I have faltered

Am I the only one to see what I see
Surely other travelers couldn' t miss
Or are they blinded 'cause the Lord chose me
There is no other reason not to notice

The clouds parted, the sun shined, and the gates showed
Who would have thought you can drive to Heaven on an asphalt road

A Bit More Mature

IF TOMORROW WAS YOUR LAST DAY...

Would you?
Would you freeze solid as panic struck like lightning paralyzing your very movement?
    Would you?
    Would you cry yourself into a fetal position in the exact place, the exact space that you learned the news?
Would you?
Would you slow your body as your thoughts race faster and faster to a velocity you cannot comprehend?
    Would you?
    Would you ask, Why? and then why again, and again, and again, and again?
Would you?
Would you beg forgiveness for a life time of wrongs?
    Would you?
    Would you crash the world around you in ire be cause others deserve this fate more than you?
Would you?
Would you plead to the air for just a little longer, one more day even, as desperation poured down your face like sweat?

Would you?
Would you gaze somberly as a blanket of reality fell over you restricting your inhale at that moment?

Would you?
Would you tell the people you love that you love them?

Would you?
Would you rush to put your affairs in order concocting a will for the loyal few?

Would you?
Would you breathe in admiring the immediate world around as if someone pressed a slow motion button?

Would you?
Would you remain poised, unfazed, smiling knowing it is the quality, not the quantity, of life you were put here for?

Would you?
Would you continue on with your usual daily routine as if that door had never opened because you have a deeper understanding that no person should ever be privy to this information?

Would you?
Would you peak with curiosity craving the unobtainable knowledge of what lies on the other side?

Answer Then Question

Would you?
Would you burst with rejoice for the Lord's word preaches that death, not life, is the true beginning?
    Would you?
    Yes. I would.

A Bit More Mature

LOOK UP...

In pain
I stand alone
And I look up
It is up that comforts me
And aids me in my pain

A Bit More Mature

LOVE WELL...

Can' t see the bottom
Can' t hear the bottom
You see me with two pails
And wonder why I got them
I tether the pails
And lower them slow
With what will I fill?
From down, down below
You will see soon
It will be quite obvious
It is a gift
Shared by both of us
I' m raising the line
You can' t wait to see
Oh how you wonder
What could it be?
Be patient
The pails are almost up
Just be prepared
To hold out your cup
Excitement
Anticipation

I assure you
It's a wonderful sensation
You will know it
I won't have to tell
I'll give you a hint
It is called the 'Love Well'

MEASURE OF A MAN...

Ability to say 'No' and still be considered kind
Knows when to quiet and when to speak his mind
Has a look that commands respect even in silence
Quick to offer a hand or words of guidance
Keeps a proper blend of masculine with a touch of gentle
Has strength equal part physical equal part mental
Bleeds with compassion while still looking tough
Has a family scale of forgiveness that reads 'Never Enough'
Is followed in the absence of talking
Is followed just by his walking
Makes people laugh in jest but when firm beware
When it comes to friends there is loyalty to spare
Remains calm and decisive in the midst of chaos
Offers comments of empathy to those suffering loss
May be afraid but does not demonstrate fear
When greeted with adversity will always persevere
Confronts the masses when he believes what is right
Secures his family and home on every given night
Even when not present people recall his sound
Loved ones share his stories long after he's in the ground
More than a cliché
He shows greatness over a lifetime
Not just for one day

A Bit More Mature

MMA...

MMA is Mixed Martial Arts
It is not 'Cage Fighting'
Not fighting in a cage
To aggressors in rage
It is a fenced in venue
A place to demonstrate art into
It is not two thugs who can' t hold down a job
Guys who lie, beat women, and rob
Not menaces to society
Misfits of the worst variety
Not a destiny for men with a short fuse
All about Mohawks and seedy body tattoos
It is not a contest of poor anger management
Barbarians sent
To unleash pent up childhood frustration
People better served locked up in segregation
It is not two meanies looking to kill
Void of all skill
That can' t feed their ego in any other way than a violent thrill
It is not an attempt to impress a girl
Develop a monster ego

A Bit More Mature

And a swelled head
Glorified blood shed
Fighting to the death
Until someone is dead
It is not a forum for the uneducated
Display of ignorance
Making reference
To being punch drunk
Or too stupid to do anything else other than punch
someone in the face
A primitive example of the human race
Not even a trace
Or sign of intelligent life
What else could a fighter do other than fight?
Nothing. Absolutely nothing.
What do you expect from someone who does Cage
Fighting?
I told you before it is not Cage Fighting
Now who is not so bright?
Do I need to turn up your lighting?
It is an honorable, sanctioned sport
Intelligence and competition in short
It is chess with a body part
A masterpiece of moving art
A demonstration of skill and heart
Separating exceptional from good apart
Culmination of mind, body, and emotion

Alphas in motion
Darwinism based on practice and perseverance
Adherence
To a life style of dedication
A sensation
That keeps one striving for perfection
In not one but a multitude of areas
A blending of creativity with tradition
An individual mission
To test oneself
It is learning in victory
And learning more in defeat
What to improve upon
What not to repeat
Growth as a competitor
Growth as a person
Building of character
Honor, trust, friendship, sportsmanship, hardship
No ego trip
But camaraderie, integrity, fraternity
When presented with a challenge
It is calculating a remedy
It is adaptable knowledge with real world application
Not just for self-defense in a physical altercation
Problem solving
Trying a new intervention
Thinking outside of the box

For a better conclusion
Method of managing stress
Learning to accomplish more by doing less
Not just making do with what you got
But enhanced training so you may achieve a lot
Establishing confidence
And self-worth
Taking pride in what you do
Giving reason to be placed on this Earth
You see a violent, mindless activity
I see a mindful display of training and ingenuity
One last thought I have to say
End your stereotype on this day
And develop an appreciation for MMA

PAIN OF ALL PAINS...

My spirit is spent
My insides now hollow
I cannot produce tears
Nor can I swallow
    I have only two thoughts
    Disbelief and why
    No one can answer me
    They just hug me and sigh
Home after work
Will never be the same
I don' t know who
But someone is to blame
    My love turns to anger
    Half of me is lost
    Why is it I
    Who pays such a cost?
Lord what have I done?
I do not understand
Neighborhood walks are painful
With nothing in my hand
    No more park
    Or Saturday mornings
    God I feel empty
    I really miss those things

One month has passed
And I finally cried
I will never recover
From the day my daughter died

RISE UP...

Experience
My teacher
Consequence
My guide
Abide
As if by law
I saw
Wisdom
In a nearby elder
Helped me discover
My days
My ways
And how to conquer this world
Not just skim by
I try
To be significant in everything
Sing a song that has not yet been sung
Reach for the top rung
Normal unwanted
Average unacceptable
Be reputable
By showing leadership
Don' t be a drone

A Bit More Mature

Stand alone
If there is no one else at the top
Don't drop
To a lesser level
Revel
In the absence of company
Be all you can be
Like in the Army
Minus the bugles and conformity
No points for similarity
Only originality
Listen to me
See
I know what I am talking about
Because with my binoculars I look out
I find I am by myself

sob**Eric**...

Hard times in the past
And will be again
I have new strength
To the Lord I say, 'Amen'

I once adopted the poison
For I knew it all too well
Now I climb the ladder
Out of that personal hell

New insight, wisdom, and weapons
I use for battle every day
I would like to say it is easy
But that I cannot say

This will always be my demon
From day's beginning till day's end
The Lord has prepared me diligently
So I am sure this is a war I will win

A Bit More Mature

SOLITARY CONFINEMENT...

The designment
Of solitary confinement
Is by definition nothing
Sounds easy, even harmless
Unless
You have a body and mind to maintain
Then it produces an agonizingly dull pain
I have thoughts that will never come to fruition
Arrested ambition
Purgatory I' ve stumbled upon
The concept of future tense- gone
I can tell it won' t be long before I go insane
With nothing significant to stimulate my brain
The differentiation of time bleeds seamlessly together
When I lack a clock and changes in weather
How to occupy my time is a full time job
I stare at a door but cannot locate a door knob
The silence is deafening
I never understood that adage until my bestowed sentencing
Now I know it far too well
It is a perpetual, quiet hell
At first I rather enjoyed the solitude

A Bit More Mature

I've since developed a much different attitude
Now. No.
Definitely and definitively not
I have difficulty thinking my next thought
I write to occupy my time and existence
Needing a point of reference
To maintain my mental health
I'm struggling to take care of myself
I would beckon for help if I believed there to be an
inkling of hope
Nope.
'Not even a glimmer' as the saying sometimes goes
In here I have a number of relentless foes
Loneliness, atrophy, silence, monotony,
The only two scents I smell have now finally gotten to me
The scent of myself and the scent of musty
The more time passes the more they disgust me
Only one vista, never changing for the rest of my life
I am starting to forget the outline of my wife
Memories faded
Beliefs in humanity jaded
An already tight space has the walls closing in
Day to day inactivity equals one me too thin
My time here has been both stagnant and spent
And not a soul that surrounds me cares that I'm innocent

Answer Then Question

STATUS QUO NO...

To move beyond status quo
How would one succeed
Simply change from yesterday
And one will succeed indeed

A Bit More Mature

THE GIFT...

Once upon a time, on a Sunday morning walk
A man was stopped mid-stride by a gentleman with talk
The man spoke softly, he had some thoughts to share
He was a thin man with a hood that covered his hair
 "I speak of a gift that makes a life worth living
You must find this 'gift' , for it is one I am not giving
Understand my words, do not just hear what I say
For if you do not understand I cannot show you the way"
 "What is this gift and where can it be found?
Can I find it in walking distance or is it outside of town?
Quick strange man do not delay, share with me this news
I need some direction and I have not a moment to lose!"
 "Patience eager one, for the gift is not going anywhere
No matter a day or a decade if you open the door the gift will still be there
Your journey is lengthy and the harshness thick
But the reward, I promise, is nothing short of euphoric"
So the man endured a journeyman' s journey with an inner-drive unmatched
Not even knowing his destination but to the idea he was attached
His travels had gotten him weary but never broke his will
As he reached a clearing on the mountain top his body

shivered a chill
The man looked up and behold, there stood the magical door
Such beauty to it the man could do nothing but adore
In awe he walked slowly and turned the door open
 Gave a swift pull and then, and then
   "Magical door? I see not a thing, is this some kind of hoax?
Was I a fool to the strange man playing victim to his jokes?"
The hooded man appeared as if from nowhere standing side a tree
   "I' m confused strange man; I see not a gift for me!"
   "You have traveled the journey and opened the door
You have the 'gift' you need not travel any more
The gift is HOPE, one that you had already possessed
Your journey proved this, it was HOPE that let you pass the test"

WHAT I WILL DO FOR A CHILD...

I will support them at their side
I will act as their moral guide
I will teach them the golden rule
I will treat them like the crown jewel
I will instruct them to be polite and never mean
I will serve as the rock on which they may lean
I will offer them positive words whenever the need
I will demonstrate the act of giving, not the act of greed
I will give them encouragement
I will stifle discouragement
I will model turn taking and sportsmanship
I will provide them with a caring relationship
I will nurture them in times of strife
I will educate them on skills necessary for life
I will inform them of the benefits of unity
I will mold them to be a pillar of the community
I will tutor them on compassion and empathy
I will assist them with whatever they strive to be
I will listen to what they believe
I will praise them on what they achieve
I will watch as they become a success
I will have expected not anything less
I will be there
I will always be there

A Bit More Mature

WHAT IS ART...

Expression of self
Demonstration of idea
Provocation of thought
See what I see
What makes up me
As I define beauty
From achievement
To bereavement
Power, love, loneliness
Everything in between
And all the rest
No limit to the medium
I create what I absorb
And then some
Anything and everything is my motivation
Combination
Of the real and of the thought up
Manipulation
I will bring life to the unliving
Giving
Objects a pulse
They gain a soul
Take on a new role

A Bit More Mature

Of existence
Materials of circumstance
Not by chance
But by my choosing
Using
Whatever gets my passion across
To you, me
The audience
Hence
I am a vehicle
To drive forth intrigue
I'm in a league
All my own
Only I can judge
The work I've shown
You want a price tag?
It won't be a precise tag
How do you put a worth on what I conjure?
The original and obscure
I ask you for that answer
Can you dissect the value apart?
I can't
What is art?

WHERE HAS CREATIVITY GONE? ...

Searching. Perplexed.
Where went our creativity?
Is it captured in captivity?
If not stolen then stifled
Stuck, stymied, and starving
Help creativity flourish
Not hinder it
Slow going malnourish
Down with ideals of conformity
Repetition and uniformity
We need to storm the beaches of originality
Like we stormed the beaches of Normandy
No idle stance
Stagnant at a glance
Open your mind
Find and cut duplicate thoughts that align
Our brains that are imprisoned
Restricting ideas of awesomeness in abundance
Don't be wed to same and the history of redundance
Escape the norm
It is a chalice filled with lame
Doing as others do
Is an unfulfilling game
Don't play it

A Bit More Mature

I urge you not to participate
Just Say No!
Like Nancy in the eighties
I'm talking to you
Kids, teens, gentlemen, and ladies
Recycled notions can be quite contagious
We have long since passed it
So don't bring back the Dark Ages
Remember the works of Shakespeare
We need new thoughts to persevere
Enough already
We've had our fill of mediocrity
Open your imagination blinds
Take note of what you'll see
I am begging you
Please.
Surpass the minds of Socrates,
Einstein, and Hemmingway
Find a way
Thwart the repeat
For Heaven's sake
Take and stake your claim
On a new day of conception
Inception of a new era
Beware of what your neighbors do
And do not follow suit
Pick out your own clothes

Take your creativity off mute
Where has creativity gone?
No.
Where had creativity gone.

A Bit More Mature

WHO AM I...

Nine months, not me,
I was born early
I weigh a lot less than the other babies,
Wouldn't you agree?
I have tubes running to my nose,
So there is something wrong I assume
And I'm not with the rest of the babies,
I have my own special room
I'm not hungry or thirsty,
Yet I cry and I cry
I guess I want something,
But I don't know what or why?
Not only do I cry,
But I'm beginning to shake
I'm fine on the outside,
But inside I ache
Will I live?
I don't know—maybe
It's just one of the consequences I deal with
From being a crack-baby

A Bit More Mature

WILL TOMORROW BE ANOTHER TODAY...

I will not bear even one day in vain
If tomorrow offers no change then I will refrain
If boredom's on the menu, no thanks I'll abstain
For me a day of repetition produces no gain
I am never willing to endure that kind of pain
I have a plethora of activity swimming in my brain
The ideas of yesterday no longer course through my vein
It matters not if today was exciting or plain
Tomorrow I will chase new and different until I can detain
My stand is steadfast, I'm unwilling to wane
I need day to day variety to keep day to day sane
If monotony are the links then I will break the chain
I will change scenery or I will jump from the train
You ask my thoughts, and this is what I say
No, tomorrow will not be another today

A Bit More Mature

MY OOLONG...

Here lies my tea
All cozy and warm
I enjoy the taste
Light and subtle in form
Smooth as I drink
With comfort and ease
As I find the bottom
May I get a refill please?

A Bit More Mature

END TOMORROW BECOME TODAY...

I'm not having a real good day
Can anything else possibly go wrong?
Why does this day seem to be so damn long!
Why can I not get anything right?
Mistakes piling up morning, noon, and night
If this continues I might do something drastic, I just might
As I sit slumped over I cry and I wallow
My usefulness is gone, on the inside I'm hollow
I am now out of tears, and I also can't swallow
I track thoughts of death and I want to follow
Out of the three hundred sixty-five days selected
Three hundred sixty-five of them I was corrected
I am a problem that's been overtly detected
I do not feel even the slightest bit protected
I am the epitome of lost and rejected
Tomorrow I will end it all...
Tomorrow is now today so here's a little news brief
When I woke up this morning I breathed a sigh of relief
Today I will put a new plan into action
I'm changing up everything so I get a completely different reaction
My goal from now on is self-satisfaction
See, I realized I was carrying unnecessary weight

A Bit More Mature

Now I know that it is never too late
To set a new standard and make my own fate
From this point forward I will only cater to a world to which I create
So here is the here and now of this situation
I'm done being the only cast of alienation
I've since come to a brand new formulation
I never again want to feel that incompetent, bottom-feeding sensation
You are now about to witness my whole new revelation
Today I will begin it all...

SECOND TO THE WOMB...

I' ve been trying since day one
To compete for the love of my son
But I' m no match
For how they are attached
It' s a different kind of history, you see
He had nine more months with her than he had with me
Nine months over a life time may not seem like very much
But it is the quality of that time, that bond, that I could never touch
Jealous? No. Absolutely not.
It' s just one of God' s gifts that she possesses and I do not
To witness that symbiotic touch
Is a miracle in motion
Consider the notion
Of two people
As one whole
Sharing the same soul
Connected on every level
Every point
A joint collection
One direction
Love
Unequalled love

A Bit More Mature

It cannot be explained
It cannot be taught
It cannot be trained
It is what it is
Heaven's mystery
At least that's what I see
When I revel in their relationship
I know I haven't been where they've been
I'm on the outside looking in
Green with envy, yeah you would assume
But no, I'm perfectly okay with being second to the womb

Answer Then Question

Juvenilia

Chapter 4
Juvenilia

Juvenilia

A GHOST NOSE...

A ghost knows
That a ghost nose
May or may not be useful
So it weighs the cons
Then it weighs the pros
And then sees how the face goes

Juvenilia

BAGEL...

The day is still early but already such a drag
Why am I at the bottom of this tight fitting bag?
I'd move to the top of the bag if I got my wish
Down here, I've got one word for you, and that word is
 "squish"
Before I was dropped in, I was fluffy and rounded
Now with blokes on top of me, I am smashed and grounded
I dream of the day I pop from the toaster with ease
And get smothered on top with a blanket of cream cheese
Hot and fresh on a plate next to a tall glass of juice
We'll set it off up in this party when we get loose
And if the fruit shows up, consider this your warning!
You will be dancing for joy on this Tuesday morning!

Juvenilia

BOMBS AWAY...

Bombs away
Bombs away
Yes indeed
On any given day
Why would I want them near?
Do you think I enjoy living in fear?
Who would want them close?
My guess would be not most
Does anyone disagree?
Don' t know about you
But I know it' s not me!
They drop and go boom!
Keep them far from my room!
Bombs away
Bombs away
Always!
Every day!

Juvenilia

BRACES? ...

As I stared at my mom and made silly faces
She stared back and said, "Son, I think you need braces."
  "What!" I claimed. "What on Earth are you talking about?"
  "Well, your teeth are a bit crooked and some stick out."
I said, "How can I be a boy to admire
When I have a mouth all riddled with steel wire!"
Mom said, "Stop with your problem and think of the goal."
I yelled. "You won' t be the one that looks like a troll!"
She replied, "You will soon have a mouth with straight teeth,
Just like your older cousins both Justin and Keith."
I muttered, "The kids are still going to tease me."
  "You will thank me even if it won' t be easy."
  "Alright, alright," I said, "I' ll give braces a try.
But the humiliation might cause me to die.
I' m still not happy if you didn' t get my gist."
She said, "Hurry up, you' ll be late for the dentist!"
The dentist walked in, "Hi, I am Doctor Horner,
Please sit and relax in the chair in the corner.
I will be the one to straighten up your bright smile."
Oh great, this is going to take quite a while.
The poking and pulling had already begun
I only just got here and wasn' t having fun

Juvenilia

Now nearly finished I was dreading the public
The thought of my friends seeing me made me feel sick
Now at school, I didn't want them to see me talk
My friends stared at me blankly, as in total shock
Then Lisa said, "You got braces, that is so cool!"
What? Was she joking with me? I feel like a fool.
She then said, "I'm not able to get braces yet.
I hope, like you, they are something I someday get!"
Then Phil said, "You got braces! That is really great!
I'm supposed to this summer, I can hardly wait."
This can't be happening? Do they all think this way?
And I was prepared for an embarrassing day.
Wow, all the kids are envious of my braces?
Soon they will appear on all of my friends' faces
 "Hey Mom guess what, my friends didn't tease me at all,
And some kids are getting their own braces this fall.
 "Mom, I am sorry I was hard on you before.
I may not even doubt you as much anymore."

CHAIR...

Butts, and butts, and lots more butts
That is all I ever see
And a dozen times a day
People sit all over me
Some I can barely notice
Oh so skinny and so light
While others push my limits
Squeezing till my arms are tight
Folks come and go, go and come
You got up for food four times
And did not offer me some
I do not just support you
I am fine furniture art
So please think of that next time
Before you sit down and fart!

Juvenilia

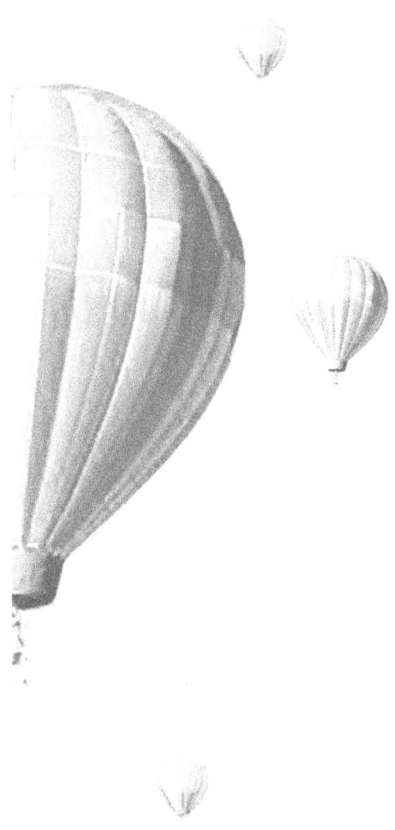

CLOCK...

I must be popular, everyone's always looking my way
Even when I am sick, I am accurate two times a day
I guess I look pretty good, based on all of the folks staring
It is either my strong hands, or the cool numbers I'm wearing
People cannot live without me, they need me all of the time
With my smooth tick and tock, and frequent, helpful alarming chime
You know I always deliver, no worries about my size
I am obviously smart, they boast of me turning "clockwise"
I'm swiftly at the ready, every morning, noon, and night
So if you need to know the when, I'll certainly do you right

Juvenilia

CURIOSITY KILLED THE CAT...

Shame on you Curiosity! That is not okay!
What did that cute, harmless cat do to you anyway?
Have you not heard? Violence is never the answer
It is not polite to kill things all covered in fur
Killing is so wrong, I do not know where to begin
Let's start with orange jump suits and decades in prison!
If you feel upset, ask The Cat to apologize
It is too late to problem solve after The Cat dies
Let's change it to be: Curiosity Kissed The Cat
It's a nicer ending, how can you argue with that?

Juvenilia

DOG EAT DOG WORLD...

Dog eat dog world? Sounds like a terrible place
Who's heard of a world where you eat your own race?
The whole idea is really unnerving
Do dogs eat nice dogs or ones more deserving?
Dogs eating other dogs sounds so very cruel
Once all of the dogs are gone, will the cats rule?
Why each other and not delicious dog food?
Eating your friends is simply gross, and it's rude
If dogs are gone who will we walk in the park?
And no other animal knows how to bark
Who will we play fetch with again and again
When there no longer is our "Man's best friend?"
No more tails wagging. No droopy eyes sagging.
What? No more fat dogs to pull in a wagon!
I cannot bare the thought, it makes me upset
To even consider my pet ate my pet!
This isn't normal, in fact, strangely bizarre!
Let's do something before madness goes too far!
We cannot let this awful idea go
Or tomorrow no Spot and then no Fido!
I'll change it from Dog Eat Dog to Dog Eat Bone
So all our dogs will live to be fully grown

Juvenilia

BE THANKFUL FOR WHAT YOU DON'T HAVE...

Be thankful for what you don' t have

   Like a face covered in blue Chicken Pox
   Or a large pillow full of river rocks
   Maybe a bag of someone' s dirty socks
Be thankful for what you don' t have

   Like forty toes crowding each of your feet
   Or a cold dinner of salty green meat
   Maybe a garden on a busy street
Be thankful for what you don' t have

   Like a cannon pointed straight at your head
   Or a new life jacket made out of lead
   Maybe a thousand tacks inside your bed
Be thankful for what you don' t have

   Like a spider crawling all through your hair
   Or a spring poking from your only chair
   Maybe orange dress pants with a long tear
Be thankful for what you don' t have

Juvenilia

    Like a house sitting on a railroad track
    Or a fish tank with a great big old crack
    Maybe poison berries for a late snack
Be thankful for what you don' t have

    Like a small candle in a windy breeze
    Or a friend who sits close and likes to sneeze
    Maybe some dirt on your favorite cheese
Be thankful for what you don' t have

    So, the next time you hear someone say,
    "I' m so thankful for what I have."
    You can Be Thankful For What You Don' t Have

HIDE-AND-GO-SEEK...

Sometimes me and my dad enjoy playing Hide-And-Go-Seek
He covers both his eyes when I hide, but sometimes I peek
He counts very slowly from the first number to the last
When it is my turn to count, I try and rush through real fast
In the places he hides, he doesn't usually fit
When he says that it's my turn, I tell him I am not 'it'
He tells me the places where we are not allowed to hide
Sometimes I do not listen, and still try to sneak inside
My dad keeps on telling me that the cheaters never win
But I just keep beating him over and over again

Juvenilia

MY JUNIOR HIGH FORMAL...

There are only two weeks until the junior high formal
I am already getting nervous, I wonder, is this normal?
The big day is so quickly approaching
And I'm a hot mess in desperate need of some coaching!
Hair up? Hair down? How should I do my hair?
And for Heaven's sake, I haven't got a single thing to wear!
Sequins or ruffles? Maybe a belt and a pleat?
I then have to decide what will go on my feet!
Should the dress be strapless or over the shoulder
I don't want to look old, but just a little bit older
Down to my knees or a smidge past my calf?
A floral pattern or stripes across half?
Should I wear flats or brave something with a heel?
I like ruby red, but I also like teal
Now I need to practice my smile and photograph stance
And I guess it might be smart to actually learn how to dance
The dance is so soon, nearly moments away!
How should I act? What should I say?
Is this really the gym? It looks nothing of the sort
It is so beautiful; you'd never know it to be a basketball court
All these decorations and wonderful flowers
This seems like a perfect place to pass the next three hours
I see my friends in the corner being monitored by teachers

But is he here? Yes he is! Over there next to the bleachers!
Should I ask him to dance or just hope he asks me?
Not sure if it shows, but I am anxious as can be
Now he is walking over towards the punch
I will casually wander over and get some pretzels to munch
He noticed me! He noticed me! I finally got his attention!
I kind of like his tie, is that something I should mention?
Well here goes nothing, I can' t believe I' m doing this
I hope the connection between my brain and my mouth doesn' t go amiss
   "Hey, your hair looks neat."   Ah! That sounded so not cool!
Every time I open my mouth I sound like a complete fool!
This night isn' t going anything like I thought
I' m sure he wants to dance with me now-NOT!
I should definitely stop talking and just pour a punch drink
Maybe if I pour slowly it will give me a moment to think
   "Would you like to dance?"   What? Is this for real?
He is asking me, I wonder if he feels the same way I feel?
   "Yes! Absolutely! I mean yeah, okay."
This could possibly be the world' s greatest day
My mother was right when she said, "Go have fun and be worry free,
Remember to be who you are, not the people you see."
Who would have thought something good could actually come from school
My junior high formal turned out to be an evening truly magical

MY MONSTER SMELLS LIKE BROWNIES...

Not all monsters are troublesome and bad
Not all monsters are unfriendly and mad
Not all monsters are dirty and gross
Not all monsters sneak up real close
Not all monsters are evil and mean
Not all monsters are grimy and green
Not all monsters have sinister eyes
Not all monsters are gigantic in size
Not all monsters have big claws and fight
Not all monsters have long drool and bite
Not all monsters growl and make noise
Not all monsters eat little kids' toys
Not all monsters are stinky and hairy
Not all monsters are nasty and scary
Not all monsters hide deep in the dark
Not all monsters have teeth like a shark
Not all monsters keep kids from sleeping
Not all monsters are lurking and creeping
MY monster is loving and nice as can be
I hope you get a great monster just like me

Juvenilia

WHOSE TOES ARE THOSE? ...

Whose toes are those,
Attached to them feet?
I'm not sure when they got here
But I find them to be neat
I thought them feets were something
But toes, who would've thought
Look at all my little piggies
That I just now got
Not sure what they do
Or why they showed up here
I think they'll keep me occupied
At least until next year
I just got these new toys
And mom covers them with a sock
If I only knew some words
Me and mom would have a talk

Juvenilia

I WANNA WOOLY WALLET...

I wanna wooly wallet to keep my money in
I wanna wooly wallet that is paper-thin

I wanna wooly wallet so made out of wool
If I had a wooly wallet boy would I be cool

A wild, wooly, wallet, is the one for me
I would keep in my wallet a bill made out of three

I wanna wanna wooly wanna wild wooly wallet
I weally wanna wooly wallet, I don' t have one yet
If I had a wild wooly wallet then the friends I' d get

I got to, get to, go to, I' m going to the store
To buy my wooly wallet that costs dollars four

Oh boy! Oh boy! Hey mom, look what I done get
I spendid all my money, I' ll be forever in a debt
But that' s okay mom, I got my WOOLY WALLET

Juvenilia

NIGHT...

I see the darkness
But I envision the light
And that is what keeps me
Unafraid of the night

Juvenilia

NUMBERS ALONE...

1 and 2, and 3 but not 4
4 was insulted and then shown the door
5 and 6, but doubts about 7
You don' t fit with us, go hang with 11
There' s 8 with 9, who were just using 10
How difficult it can be, to just have a friend

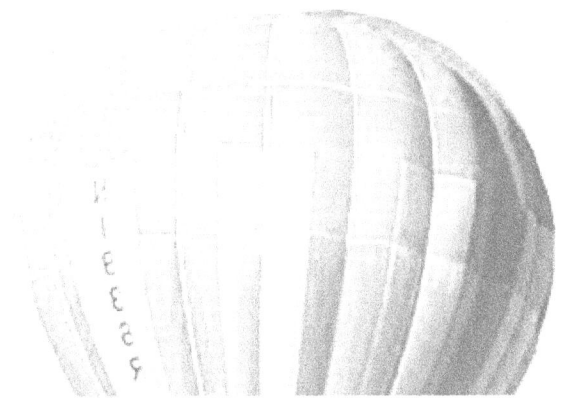

Juvenilia

ON CLOUD NINE...

Why would someone pick cloud nine?
Why would someone choose that one?
Is it softer than others?
Is it a whole lot more fun?

Why would you stop at this cloud?
Why not stop at one through eight?
What is it about cloud nine
That makes that one so darn great?

I wonder who made cloud nine?
Quite a novel creation
Is it a serious place?
Or more like a vacation?

What's with all the brouhaha?
I think I would like to go
Are there more clouds after nine?
Maybe hundreds in a row?

I think I like, "On Cloud Ten"
That's what I'm going to say
I would choose ten over nine
On each and every day

Juvenilia

PHONE...

Please be easy on my buttons as you press
I'm kind of sensitive, I must confess
Every now and again untangle my cord
I will let you talk farther away as your reward
Let me ring a bit, I have an awesome ring tone
It is not my fault that you are always alone
And if you take a moment to move your '80s hairdo out of the way
You may just hear what the other person has to say
Boy, those earrings that keep bumping me are tacky and gaudy
And why do you move your hands while you talk, if no one can see your body?
Whoa! Close talker, close talker, please move back
If I was any closer to your mouth I would be an afternoon snack
And if you plan on getting that close, let's try a few breath mints
Can you clean your hands please? I'm allergic to fingerprints
All day long I am glued to your ear
I'm surprised at this point that you can even still hear
And what is it with all that pacing and squeezing?

Juvenilia

For your information this level of stress isn' t too pleasing
What is this thing with the head and shoulder pinch?
When you remove your hand I get all worried and flinch
Sneezing! Really! You couldn' t use your arm to deflect
At the very least take a moment to help me disinfect
One more thing you could kindly do for me
When finished hang me up ever so gently

PICKLE...

How humiliating, being dropped in a jar by a stork
Then the occasional poking by a finger or a fork
My goodness! Move over please!
I cannot wait until one of you guys leaves
The less crowded the better, I am sure everyone agrees
I would rather hang out with Tomato Soup and his pal Grilled Cheese
I didn't mind so much being cut into quarter
But the way we get picked has no particular order
This is by far the strangest liquid I have ever seen
The pool started out clean but each day turns more green
I would visit my parents, if I were granted one wish
But I cannot because I am Kosher, and they are both Polish
Everyone keeps getting picked, when is it my turn to win
I long for the day to be on a plate with Reuben

Juvenilia

PRESIDENT DUCK...

You would think the life of a duck is easy, what's not to love? But no one cares about us, we're always being made fun of You name some wise cracks, and I will bet that I have heard them all
 "Knee-high to a duck" they say, that means you are not very tall
 "Look at them big, goofy, webbed feet" they always seem to muddle
 "No wonder he keeps them feet at the bottom of a puddle"
 "Excuse me mister duck, would you care for 'quackers' with your cheese?"
 "Will you pay cash or should I just put it on your bill?" they tease
They are always yelling to me, "Like water off a duck's back"
I don't know what that means, but I know it is some kinda crack
Someday they will respect ducks, and they will not make jokes at me
That is PRESIDENT DUCK to you fellow, just you wait and see!

Juvenilia

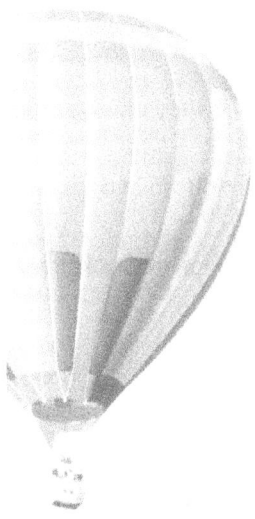

SHORT ON TIME...

Short on Time, I do not think I understand
If Short is on Time, how on Earth does Time stand?

Why doesn't someone tell Short, to get off Time?
Wouldn't it be assault? Or some kind of crime?

Is Time ever on Short? Or is Short too tall?
Never mind I remembered, 'short' says it all

If Short is short, how does it get way up there?
If Time's always on bottom, that isn't fair

It would be 'Short with Time', if you would ask me
Then they would be close, and friendly as can be

Juvenilia

SIOUX SAID...

Hello white man
Welcome to our land
What can we do you for?
    Yours no more
    Move it over there
    Take your stuff if you care
Why so?
We don' t want to go
Why should we have to flee?
    Us white folk agree
    We now claim this space
    Here' s a small plot for your race
Welcomed you this day
This is how you repay
Your gratitude is nil
    You bring your will
    But lack in kind
    Your fairness surely blind
You take by force
Please change your course
What have we done to you?

Juvenilia

SMELLY PEE...

Oh my, I cannot believe I have smelly pee!
I wonder what on Earth possibly causes thee?
Not all the time just every now and again
Hmmm, I'm not sure of the what, the why, or the when
I need the answer to this perplexing riddle
Is it what I do, or eat, or in the middle?
It happens after I eat, so what could it be?
I'll experiment, I'll eat, and then I'll go pee!
Not hot dogs or ice cream, meatloaf, or celery
Not peanuts or pizza, waffles, or broccoli
I wish I could know with absolute certainty
What causes me the occasional smelly pee
Does it just happen to me or any of us?
I think it's a topic we should further discuss
My conclusion still remains quite ambiguous
I'll be in my garden picking asparagus

Juvenilia

VERY BESTEST FRIEND...

I am pleased to say that we are very close
You are a true pal that I like much more than most
We watch television together from morning till noon
We also share the same favorite early morning cartoon
We have sleepovers and look out at the moon and the stars
Then we set up our flashlights to play with my little toy cars
Sometimes we read together or run around on the basketball court
Other times we play army and hide out in our secret fort
You were there for me when I lost my first tooth
We had fun getting our picture taken in the small photo booth
You comfort me in my times of need
Like when I scraped my knee and then started to bleed
You always help me make my long Christmas list
And you calm me down before a trip to the dentist
You celebrated with me on my kindergarten graduation
And you stay with me each and every summer vacation
We relax on the beach together as we play in the sand
When I get scared at the movies you clench tight to my hand
You watched the first time I rode with my training wheels off
You stayed beside me all night when I was sick with a cough

Juvenilia

From the day' s beginning until the day' s end
I could not ask for a better bestest friend
And one last thing before I forget
There will never be a better bestest blanket.

WATCH OUT FOR BRAIN FREEZE...

I take a big bite, then another big bite
Each time just a little bit faster
Most folks everywhere, may be unaware
That I am known as an ice cream master
It tastes so great, not foreseeing my fate
I keep on trucking along
Then it hit me, it snuck up and bit me
Something has gone terribly wrong
I have barely begun, nowhere near being done
I'm beginning to feel a bit strange
My brain needs some sun, I'm not having fun
How do I halt this unwanted change?
What is this? This miserable this?
I want it to just go away
I love Rocky Road, even served a la mode
But how long is this pain going to stay?
I won't eat one more drop, just please make it stop
Oh please! Oh please! Oh please!
I'm now feeling scorned, that I was never forewarned
About this dreaded Brain Freeze!
My face in my palms, as my head explodes bombs
This is a pain I never had felt
The throbbing is strong, but I can't pause too long

Juvenilia

My ice cream is starting to melt
I must carry on, till my cone is all gone
Like I said, I am an ice cream master
Now time to think quick, I take another big lick
Each time just a little bit faster

Answer Then Question

About The Author

Ian is a Pittsburgh native, born and raised, who grew up with two working class parents and two brothers, one older and one younger. Following straight through after high school, Ian received his undergraduate degree in Elementary Education and graduate degree in Special Education at California University of PA. Ian wears many hats and has many passions in his daily life. When Ian is not writing poetry or other material, he enjoys Mixed Martial Arts training, working with special needs children through his jobs as a Program Supervisor at a school and as an Administrative Behavior Specialist at a special needs summer camp, spending time with family, riding his motorcycle, exercising, collecting Spider-man memorabilia, fishing, camping, or being outdoors.

www.ingramcontent.com/pod-product-compliance
Lightning Source LLC
Chambersburg PA
CBHW061428040426
42450CB00007B/955